STRANGE UNSOLVED MYSTERIES

MYSTERIES OF THE MIND and THE SENSES

Strange, Unsolved Mysteries from Tor books

Mysteries of Ships and Planes
Monsters, Strange Dreams, and UFOs
Mysteries of Bizarre Animals and Freaks of Nature
Mysteries of People and Places
Ghosts, Hauntings and Mysterious Happenings
Mysteries of Space and the Universe
Strange Appearances from Beyond

STRANGE UNSOLVED MYSTERIES

MYSTERIES OF THE MIND and THE SENSES

PHYLLIS RAYBIN EMERT
Illustrated by JAEL

A TOM DOHERTY ASSOCIATES BOOK
NEW YORK

MYSTERIES OF THE MIND AND THE SENSES

Copyright © 1995 by RGA Publishing Group, Inc..

Cover and interior illustrations by Jael

A Tor book
Published by Tom Doherty Associates, Inc.
175 Fifth Avenue
New York, N.Y. 10010

Tor® is a registered trademark of Tom Doherty Associates, Inc.

ISBN: 0-812-53633-9

First edition: July 1995

Printed in the United States of America

0 9 8 7 6 5 4 3 2 1

For
Holly Corrin Kent,
Scotlyn Elizabeth Kent,
and
Jacob Mitchell Kent

Contents

Premonitions of Disaster   1

Burned Alive   6

Talking Objects   10

Destination Unknown   14

Head and Hands   17

A Nightmare to Remember   20

Warning or Coincidence?   25

Reborn   28

Avoiding Disaster   33

Spirit Writing   38

Murder in the House   43

The Gypsy's Prediction   47

Contents

The Man with the X-ray Eyes   51

Danger at Sea   55

Sounds from the Past   59

Glimpse of the Future   63

Bad Dream   69

Past Lives   72

The Next Voice You Hear   77

Dream of Bill   81

Hidden History   84

The Flying Friar   89

Future Lives   94

The Gift   100

Collision!   105

Psychic Detective   108

Glossary   112

Bibliography   119

Premonitions of Disaster

Certain psychic individuals receive advance warning or knowledge of an event before it actually happens. This is called a premonition or precognition, and can occur in the form of a dream, a strong feeling, or an overpowering vision.

Even more amazing is when dozens of unrelated individuals have similar premonitions of the same, single disaster. This is exactly what happened in an incident described by Herbert B. Greenhouse in his book *Premonitions: A Leap into the Future*.

Beginning in mid-October of 1966, dozens of people living in England began feeling nervous and uneasy. On October 14, a man named Alexander Venn remarked to his wife, "Something terrible is going to happen, and it won't be far from here." According to Greenhouse, Venn couldn't stop thinking about coal dust.

Three days later, another man felt there would be a horrible disaster and that it would occur on Friday. The feeling was so strong he told a girl in his office, "On Friday, something terrible connected with death is going to happen."

On Thursday night, October 20, several people in different areas of England dreamed of being smothered in blackness. Earlier that morning, nine-year-old Eryl Mai Jones told her mother about a strange dream she had. "I went to school," she said, "and there was no school there. Something black had come down over it." At the same time, a woman named Mrs. C. Milden had a haunting vision of a small school in a valley and "an avalanche of coal rushing down a mountainside."

On the morning of Friday, October 21, Sybil Brown awoke after having a nightmare of a child followed by a black mass. She told her husband, "Something terrible will happen." Simultaneously, a man had a strange dream in which a bright light spelled out A-B-E-R-F-A-N.

Little did the man know that there was a tiny village in South Wales called Aberfan. Aberfan was located in a valley at the base of a mountain. According to Greenhouse, Pantglas Junior School was located six hundred feet below the top of the mountain, which was used as a dumping ground for huge amounts of coal waste from the nearby mines.

At 9:15 on that same Friday morning, Monica McBean had a sudden vision of a "black mountain moving and children buried under it." Moments later, the mountain of coal waste, weighing one million tons and reaching forty feet high, roared down the slope and completely buried the school, a row of terraced houses, and a farm that had stood in its way.

Many of those who had premonitions of the disaster didn't hear the tragic news until later that day or the next morning. Out of 144 people who died, 116 of them were children. One of those children was Eryl Mai Jones.

In a survey done after the Aberfan tragedy by J. C. Barker, a London psychiatrist, almost two hundred people claimed they had

premonitions of the disaster. They either had a dream, a vision, or a feeling that something horrible was going to happen. Were all two hundred claims valid premonitions? Was it just coincidental that so many people had similar feelings of disaster?

Dr. Barker believes certain psychic people sense upcoming calamities, similar to the way a seismograph records movements of the earth in earthquakes. Can these human seismographs actually predict future catastrophes? And if they can, will people take them seriously? Would you?

Burned Alive

She dreamed the hotel room was in flames. There was no escape from the blazing inferno. The heat was unbearable.

"Help!" she screamed. "Somebody help me!"

The burning smoke seared her throat, and her lungs felt as if they were ready to explode. She gasped for air, but whatever oxygen remained was consumed by the fire.

Just before losing consciousness, the woman looked down and saw tendrils of flame lick at the hem of her long nightgown.

"I will be burned alive," she thought to herself, "and no one can help me." Then she

felt terrible pain and heat, and finally, a merciful blackness.

The woman woke up in a sweat. She looked around nervously and then felt a huge wave of relief. "It was only a dream," she said aloud to the empty room. But then the woman became alarmed, for she realized the dream had taken place in that very hotel room! She became frightened. "If I stay here," she thought, "I will die a horrible death."

When the woman got up the next morning, she told her niece, who was traveling with her, about the dream. "We must pack at once," she said, "and go back to Philadelphia."

The two were visiting Atlantic City, New Jersey, in the late 1800s on the advice of a doctor. The woman had looked forward to a restful vacation, relaxing in the sun and breathing the sea breezes along the boardwalk.

Disturbed by the awful dream, the woman and her niece left Atlantic City immediately. The very next day the hotel in which they had stayed, as well as ten others and miles of the boardwalk, were destroyed by fire!

The woman in the hotel room was none other than Susan B. Anthony (1820–1906), the co-leader, along with Elizabeth Cady Stanton, of the women's suffrage movement in America, founded in 1869. First a supporter of temperance (a movement to stop the drinking of all alcoholic beverages), Anthony later worked to abolish slavery. After the Civil War, she became a leader for women's rights and concentrated her efforts on winning the vote for women until her death.

How could Anthony have known there would be a terrible fire? Was it a genuine premonition, an advance warning of an event before it happened, or just an unusual coincidence?

The horror of being burned alive was so frightening and distressing that Anthony, always known for her persistence and determination, didn't hesitate to act quickly. She was able to change the outcome of her dream by leaving the city, although the devastating fire still took place.

Had Anthony not had this premonition, the voting rights of women in America might have turned out differently. A psychic experience or a random incident? Whatever it was, it saved her life!

Talking Objects

Do all objects have a record of their own history? Do things such as rocks, walls, jewelry, items of clothing, and even locks of hair record information about animals, people, places, or events? Can certain psychic individuals obtain this information simply by being in contact with these objects?

For those who believe in psychometry, the answers are "Yes" to all of the above. Psychometry is the ability to hold an object and read its history. Colin Wilson, in his book *Beyond the Occult*, describes an experiment conducted by psychologist Lawrence LeShan in 1964 with the well-respected medium

Eileen Garrett (1893–1970). Garrett was said to be gifted in psychometry—as well as in clairvoyance, telepathy, precognition, and other extrasensory perception (ESP) abilities.

LeShan clipped a lock of hair from his twelve-year-old daughter's head, obtained some hair from the tail of his new neighbor's dog, and picked a rosebud from his garden. LeShan placed each item in a clear plastic box and told Mrs. Garrett what each box contained.

A solid partition or divider with a small hole in the middle had been set up in a room. LeShan sat on one side of the partition, while Garrett sat on the other side and put her arm through the hole. LeShan chose one of the boxes and placed it in her hands. Each could hear, but could not see the other.

Garrett immediately identified LeShan's daughter's hair and went on to correctly describe the child she had never met or seen. "I think I'll call her Hilary," said Garrett. "She'll like that." LeShan remembered that eight years before, his then four-year-old daughter, Wendy, wanted to change her name to Hilary, after a best friend. Garrett then correctly described her love of horses and interest in American history.

Garrett identified the dog hair next and declared the dog had had terrible pain in his paw. Later, LeShan's neighbors verified that several months before, the dog had cut its paw so badly it got infected and the animal was hospitalized for six weeks.

Finally, when Garrett identified the rose, she explained the soil was too acidic for it to grow well. LeShan confirmed this since his gardener had told him the exact same thing.

Was Garrett reading LeShan's mind, picking up his telepathic thoughts? It's possible in the case of his daughter's hair and the rosebud. But LeShan had no knowledge of his new neighbors or their dog, so no telepathic link was possible. Therefore, LeShan concluded Garrett must have obtained the information about the dog from its hair clipping using her skills in psychometry.

In a later experiment, LeShan gave Garrett a small square of cloth from the shirt of a missing doctor, who had gone to a medical conference and never returned home. All Garrett was told was that the doctor had disappeared. After holding the cloth a few moments, Garrett declared, "He is in La Jolla, California, the place where his father disappeared when he was fourteen."

LeShan telephoned the missing doctor's

wife that night and discovered that the doctor's father had in fact deserted his family when the doctor was fourteen years old. After a few days, the doctor returned home and verified that he had been in La Jolla, just as Garrett had said.

How did she do it? LeShan believed that mediums like Mrs. Garrett see the world completely differently than other people. Garrett herself described her experience as a "withdrawal of consciousness from the outer world, pushing the five senses to the subconscious, and seeking to focus awareness on the timeless, spaceless field of the superconscious."

Is psychometry possible? It certainly seemed so in the case of Eileen Garrett, who was highly regarded by the scientific community throughout her life.

Destination Unknown

Mysterious unexplained incidents occur in everyday life and are often remembered years later in vivid detail. One such incident was described by Louisa Rhine in her book *The Invisible Picture*.

A schoolteacher in Northern California, who shall be called Ann, drove back and forth from Walnut Creek to her job in Richmond, approximately 120 miles away. On the way, she picked up her friend Nancy, who worked in a laboratory along the route.

One particular afternoon, Ann left school extremely exhausted after a hectic day and a boring faculty meeting. After picking up

Nancy, her friend mentioned she had also had a bad day. "Would you mind if I don't talk," she asked, "but just lean back and close my eyes?"

Ann thought Nancy did look especially tired and even a bit sad as she shut her eyes and leaned back in the seat. Ann drove away and got on the freeway for the ride home.

The next thing Ann remembered was coming to a stop on a quiet street she had never seen before. She found herself parked in front of a plain brown house with brown pillars and diamond-shaped glass in the front door.

"How did I leave the freeway? Where am I?" thought Ann to herself. "Ordinarily, my route home never varies."

"Nancy," said Ann. "Open your eyes. I seem to have made a wrong turn somewhere. I think we're lost."

Nancy sat up straight and looked at the brown house. Suddenly, an expression of happiness came over her face. "I was born in that house," she said, "and spent the happiest times of my life there!"

Nancy turned to look at Ann. "I was sitting here thinking about it and longing to see it again," she said. "I haven't been back since I was a little girl. How could you have known?"

The two women stared at each other without speaking. How could Ann have driven to a place of which she had no knowledge? "Could I have read your mind and followed your directions here?" asked Ann.

"I couldn't have given you any directions. When I was a child, there was no freeway," replied Nancy. "I don't even remember any of these streets and my eyes have been closed since we left the lab."

The women sat in silence for a few minutes before Ann finally drove away. She asked directions to get back to the freeway and then drove slowly home to Walnut Creek. Ann figured she had driven fifteen to twenty blocks out of her way.

A few days later, when Ann was alone, she tried to retrace the route to the house. "I went up and down street after street," Ann said. "I never found the brown house on that quiet street again."

Did Ann use telepathy to read Nancy's thoughts of her happy childhood home, even though she wasn't consciously aware of it? Maybe so.

Yet, how could Ann have gotten there if Nancy herself didn't know the way? It remains a mystery. As Rhine states, "This case illustrates puzzling aspects that occasionally happen in life experiences."

Head and Hands

Dr. Walter Franklin Prince had a strange and disturbing dream on the night of November 27, 1917. It seemed so realistic he wrote down the details when he awoke the next morning.

Prince's dream was described by Herbert B. Greenhouse in his book *Premonitions: A Leap into the Future.* In the dream, Prince held an execution order for a woman. "The woman," Prince described, "was slender, had blond hair, small girlish features, and was rather pretty."

She seemed willing to die, but wanted Dr. Prince to hold her hand during the execution. She was ready for death without being afraid.

Suddenly, the light went out in the dream! Prince felt the woman's hand grasp his and he knew the execution was taking place at that very moment.

Next, Dr. Prince was aware of his own hand on the top of the woman's head, but was shocked to realize there was no body attached to it! His other hand became caught in the mouth of the head and its teeth opened and shut on his hand. "I was filled with the horror of a severed but living head!" Prince explained, after the dream ended.

After writing a record of the bizarre and unusual dream, Dr. Prince visited Gertrude Tubby of the American Society for Psychical Research. He described the dream to her in full. The next morning, November 29, 1917, Dr. Prince told his wife about the dream on their way to church.

That afternoon, the headline in the afternoon paper took his breath away. It read: "HEAD SEVERED BY TRAIN AS WOMAN ENDS HER LIFE."

Apparently, a woman whose name was Mrs. Hand committed suicide by putting her head on the tracks in front of a moving train. According to Greenhouse, she had left a note in her purse saying her head would continue to live on. The incident occurred less than twenty-four hours after Dr. Prince's dream and within six miles of his home. The late Mrs. Hand was described as thin, pretty, and with golden brown hair!

Did Dr. Prince have a true precognitive dream of the future? It seems so. The dream's focus on hands actually referred to the woman's name. The living head Prince described in the dream corresponds to Mrs. Hand's belief that her head would live on.

Greenhouse refers to this as a classic case of precognition because Dr. Prince had documented proof to support that his dream later came true. He had a written record before the event took place. Also, two people, Ms. Tubby and Mrs. Prince, were told about the dream and confirmed Dr. Prince's account prior to the suicide.

Did Dr. Prince's mind pick up subconscious psychic images from the mind of Mrs. Hand, like a receiver picks up radio transmissions? Do hidden mental powers exist in certain sensitive individuals?

The evidence seems to support this theory, yet no one knows absolutely. Today, much of the human mind still remains a mystery.

A Nightmare to Remember

Throughout history, dreams have influenced powerful people and significant events. In the Bible, for example, God's messages in both the Old and New Testaments (dealing with Judaism and Christianity) were revealed in dreams to Abraham, Jacob, and Joseph, husband of Mary. Dreams were also connected with the birth and life of Buddha (Buddhism)and Muhammad (Islam).

Military leaders such as Alexander the Great, Julius Caesar, and Napoleon were often influenced by their dreams. Unfortunately, Caesar disregarded a dream his wife had, as well as one by the Roman soothsayer

A Nightmare to Remember

Spurinna Vestritius, in which they both warned him to "beware the Ides of March." On this date (March 15, 44 B.C.), he was stabbed to death on the steps of the Roman Senate.

Can one particular dream affect the future of all mankind? Judge for yourself after reading an incident described in the book *Dreams and Dreaming* from Time-Life Books.

The event happened on a very cold night in November 1917, during World War I, near the Somme River in northern France. French and German soldiers were positioned in trenches on opposite sides of no-man's-land, the area that separated the two enemies from each other.

There was an unusual stillness in the air. The artillery bombardment that often continued throughout the night by both sides had stopped. A group of German soldiers took advantage of the quiet. They tried to get some sleep in the long, narrow ditch that sheltered them and protected them from enemy fire.

One German soldier had trouble sleeping. The twenty-eight-year-old corporal tossed and turned because of a terrible nightmare. He dreamed he was buried alive by earth and liquid iron and therefore choking to death. He awoke gasping for air and was very disturbed.

The young soldier knew it was a dream, but he wondered if this was how he would finally die on the battlefield. Too restless to sleep anymore, the corporal got up and went for a walk, thinking the cold, crisp air might make him feel better.

He left the protection of the trench, stepped into no-man's-land, and began walking. Unarmed, the soldier suddenly realized what an easy target he would be for a French bullet. Before he could act, gunfire erupted in the night air and a heavy artillery shell screamed overhead.

As the German dropped to his knees, the shell exploded with a thunderous boom. The gunfire stopped and the corporal ran back to the safety of the trench.

What he saw next was imprinted in his memory for the rest of his life. The French artillery shell had scored a direct hit on the trench. All that remained was dirt and rubble. The sleeping German soldiers had been killed by the explosion and buried under tons of earth.

The young corporal stood in horror as he realized he had been sleeping there only

minutes earlier. The precognitive dream had saved his life!

As the years passed, the German soldier's name and what he did came to be known throughout the world by young and old alike. He became an infamous historical figure. His terrible exploits will be taught to future generations forever.

The young corporal's name was Adolf Hitler.

Warning or Coincidence?

Everyone has experienced strange coincidences in his or her life. A man thinks of a distant relative. Seconds later, the telephone rings and that very relative is on the line.

"What a coincidence, cousin Herbert," the man exclaims. "I was just thinking of you."

A woman reminisces about a high school classmate she hasn't seen in years. The next afternoon she meets that exact person at the mall.

"I can't believe it," says the woman. "I was wondering how you were doing just yesterday."

These events may seem related, but they

have no actual connection to each other. Or do they? The following example of an amazing coincidence was described by Lyall Watson in his book *Earthworks*.

The incident occurred in March 1950, in Beatrice, Nebraska. The small church choir of fifteen people practiced in the empty church on certain days of the week at exactly 7:30 P.M. Normally, some choir members would show up early for the practice. Most would be on time, although a few might wander in a couple of minutes late. But on this particular night, a string of incredible coincidences occurred.

The organist, who was the minister's wife, was late to practice because she had to iron her daughter's dress. One young woman was finishing her math homework for school, so she was also late to practice.

Two of the men came late because they stayed a few extra minutes at their homes to catch the end of a sports broadcast on the radio. Another man took a nap and overslept. On and on went the excuses, so that not one single choir member showed up for practice on time. All fifteen members were late, and their tardiness saved their lives!

At exactly 7:25 P.M. that evening, five minutes before practice was to begin, the church was totally destroyed by a huge explosion. What were the odds that the entire choir would arrive late to practice that particular night? Incredibly slim, no doubt, because it had never happened before.

Psychiatrist Carl Jung came up with a scientific term, "synchronicity," to describe such baffling coincidences. Synchronicity is used to describe events that seem to happen for a reason but are actually not related by cause and effect.

There are those who believe that these people all came late for a reason, whether they were aware of it or not, perhaps due to extrasensory perception.

Was it merely synchronicity at work, or just a string of incredible coincidences? Or were the fifteen choir members guided by a mental warning or premonition of disaster that accounted for their lateness? Whatever the reason, after the explosion, all fifteen people were lucky to be alive!

Reborn

"I'm coming back as your next son," said Victor Vincent, a full-blooded Tlingit Indian of Alaska in 1945. He made this statement to his niece, Mrs. Corliss Chotkin. "I hope I don't stutter then as much as I do now," he declared.

Vincent showed her his scar from a past back operation, which had distinct small round holes. He also had a mark on the right side of his nose. "You'll recognize me by these scars when I come back as your son," he explained.

The Tlingit Indians believe in reincarnation—that a person's soul is reborn in a new human body after death. Vincent believed his beloved dead sister Gertrude had been reborn as Mrs. Chotkin's daughter. Others in the family believed it, too, which accounted for the fact that the child's name was Gertrude Junior. This was the reason Vincent wanted to return as his niece's son, so he could grow up again with his sister.

This case was described in detail by Ian Stevenson in his book *Twenty Cases Suggestive of Reincarnation.* Victor Vincent died a year later, in the spring of 1946. Eighteen months after his death, Mrs. Corliss Chotkin gave birth to a boy. He was named Corliss Chotkin Junior, after his father.

Strangely enough, the infant had two marks on his body almost identical to the scars pointed out by Victor Vincent prior to his death! Apart from the extraordinary birthmarks, little Corliss behaved like any other baby. However, at the age of thirteen months, when his mother was trying to teach him to say his name aloud, Corliss suddenly declared, "I'm Kahkody." This was Vincent's Tlingit tribal name. How could the toddler have known such a thing?

When Corliss was two, he recognized Vincent's stepdaughter walking along the street. "There's my Susie," Corliss stated, and also spoke her Tlingit name. On another occasion, the two-year-old spotted Vincent's son and declared, "There is William, my son."

When Corliss was three, he recognized Vincent's widow at a meeting of Tlingits and said, "That's the old lady, there's Rose." This was exactly how Vincent used to refer to his wife.

By the time young Corliss was six years old he had recognized and spoken to at least four friends of Vincent, who had walked by or near the Chotkins' home. He correctly called them all by their tribal names.

Once when Mrs. Chotkin and Corliss walked through a house the family used to live in, the boy pointed to a room and explained, "When the old lady and I used to visit you, we slept in that bedroom there." Although the room was no longer a bedroom, and the house no longer a residence, Corliss's mother verified that Victor Vincent and his wife had indeed occupied that room when they visited.

As the evidence for reincarnation began to accumulate, Mrs. Chotkin came to believe that her uncle had truly been reborn as her son. The youngster exhibited other traits similar to his dead great-uncle. He combed his hair in the same style as Vincent. He also had a severe stutter until it was partially corrected by speech therapy when he was ten years old.

Corliss was deeply religious like his great-uncle, loved boats and the water, and had a natural talent for repairing engines, just as Vincent had. However, by the time Corliss was a teenager, he had little or no memory of his supposed former life. It seemed that the older he got, the less he remembered (or chose to remember).

In an investigation of this case, Ian Stevenson confirmed that the boy's unusual birth scars coincided with the surgical scars of Victor Vincent when he was alive. Could the amazing scar and birthmark similarities have been nothing more than a remarkable coincidence?

How could young Corliss have recognized members of Vincent's family and several of his friends? Could Mrs. Chotkin have unconsciously taught her son to learn how to identify these people? It's not likely, considering Corliss's very young age at the time and Mrs. Chotkin's limited knowledge of these people.

Corliss was drafted into the army in 1968 at the age of nineteen, and served in Vietnam. He was injured in battle, suffered damage to his ears, and was then discharged. In

1972, Corliss worked as a laborer in a pulp mill in Alaska. According to Stevenson, by that time the birthmark on his nose was barely visible. The one on his back, suspected of being cancerous, was surgically removed in 1969. Only a small scar was visible.

Stevenson believed this case was suggestive of reincarnation, but there are still many unanswered questions. If it really was reincarnation, why did Corliss's memory of his former life decrease with age? Are the signs of reincarnation most visible in the earlier years of life?

Were the character traits similar to his great-uncle learned and not naturally developed, in a conscious effort to be more like Vincent? Was Corliss coached to recognize relatives and friends of his great-uncle?

Until more precise documentation and verification are available from witnesses and other reliable sources, this case of possible reincarnation, and others similar to it, will remain a mystery.

Avoiding Disaster

If certain psychic people receive advance warnings or prior knowledge of future events, can they then take steps to change what will happen? Can danger be avoided after a premonition or precognitive dream or vision?

One true case in which a terrible calamity was successfully prevented was described in *Hidden Channels of the Mind*, by Louisa Rhine. A young wife and mother, who will be called Cathy, lived in the state of Washington. One night, she had a dream so frightening that she woke up her husband, who will be called Jeff, to tell him about it.

"I dreamed that the chandelier that hangs over the crib came crashing down," Cathy said, near tears. "It crushed the baby to death." A sob caught in her throat.

"I saw you and me standing there in the baby's room. The clock said 4:35 A.M." She continued, "I could hear wind blowing and rain beating against the window. It was so real and so awful!"

Jeff comforted his wife, but couldn't help but let out a chuckle. "It's just a silly dream, Cath. It's not real." He added, "Just forget it and go back to sleep. You'll laugh about this in the morning."

Within minutes Jeff was snoring peacefully, but Cathy was too restless to sleep. She was still frightened by the vividness of the dream. She quietly slipped out of bed and walked into the baby's room. Cathy picked up her sleeping daughter from the crib.

As she carried the infant back to her bedroom, she glanced out the window. The moon was full and bright. There were few clouds in the sky and everything seemed very calm. She remembered the rain and wind in her dream.

"This is probably silly, little girl," whispered Cathy to her baby, "but you'll spend to-night with Mommy and Daddy."

Several hours later, all three were awakened suddenly by a loud crashing sound. Cathy grabbed the baby, and she and Jeff ran to the nursery. To their horror, they found the heavy, multibranched chandelier in the baby's crib. The large light fixture had come loose from the ceiling and crashed down upon the crib, breaking its sides. The massive chandelier would undoubtedly have killed the sleeping infant!

Jeff and Cathy looked at each other, too shocked to speak. Cathy pointed to the clock on the baby's dresser. It had stopped at 4:35 A.M., the exact same time as in her dream!

They stood there dumbfounded, listening to the sound of the howling wind and the noise of the heavy rain beating against the windowpanes. The calm night had changed into a raging storm.

The dream had come true in all of its details—with one exception. Cathy had removed the baby from the crib, thus saving her daughter's life. As Rhine explained, "The danger was avoided even though the rest of the event occurred," just as in the dream.

Why one person is more sensitive to psy-

chic occurrences than others is a question that remains to be answered. The ability to receive warning or knowledge from outside of the normal five senses of smell, taste, sight, touch, and hearing is one of the great unsolved mysteries of our time.

Spirit Writing

Mrs. John Curran of Saint Louis, Missouri, was skeptical about séances, mediums, and the spirit world. It wasn't until she was a thirty-one-year-old housewife that she was finally persuaded to try the Ouija board with a friend.

The popular board has the alphabet, numbers, and other symbols printed on it that are supposedly used to record and send messages to dead spirits. As the fingers of the participants rest lightly on a three-cornered device called a planchette, it spells out words while moving across the board.

Mrs. Curran and her friend, Emily

Hutchings, participated, while a third friend, Mary Pollard, recorded the letters and numbers. On July 8, 1913, the planchette moved quickly from letter to letter, spelling out the sentence "Many moons ago, I lived. Again I come—Patience Worth my name."

This marked the beginning of an amazing relationship between Curran and the spirit of Patience Worth. It lasted until Curran's death in 1937 and resulted in an outpouring of writing that astonished literary experts throughout the world. As Curran sat at the Ouija board in a trancelike state, the spirit of Patience dictated prose and poems in seventeenth-century English.

As the relationship between the two deepened, Curran was able to go into a trance without the board, and then her pen was guided by Patience directly. This was called automatic writing.

Over a number of years, Patience Worth dictated a series of six historical novels through Curran. Each novel differed in style and setting from the others, and each was highly acclaimed by critics as a great literary work. For example, *Hope Trueblood* was set in the nineteenth century, *The Sorry Tale* was about the life and times of Jesus, and

Telka was set in medieval England and actually written in Old English.

Could Curran have written the novels and poems herself and just made up the story of Patience Worth? It's not very likely. Curran had only an eighth grade education, had little knowledge of history, and wasn't well-read. The intelligence, wit, and variety of writing styles that emerged from Curran when she was guided by Patience Worth made it highly likely that a totally different person had assumed control. Many experts believe Curran could never have provided the authentic background details in Worth's historical novels.

Patience dictated to Curran so rapidly that she often wrote two or more novels simultaneously. She wrote a chapter in one and switched to a chapter in another without pausing. Patience was so productive that a monthly publication called *Patience Worth's Magazine* was published in 1918 and consisted only of dictated writings.

Who was the mysterious Patience Worth? She claimed she was born in Dorsetshire, England, during the reign of Elizabeth I (1533–1603). When she grew up, Patience and her parents moved to America. Shortly after, she was killed by an Indian war party.

Was Mrs. Curran really Patience Worth? Or was she just a medium used by a long-dead spirit? One investigator who studied the case thoroughly declared that it "must be regarded as the outstanding phenomenon of the age."

Murder in the House

John Williams had never had a psychic experience. He managed mining properties in Cornwall, England, and was a practical man who lived a normal life—until the night of May 3, 1812. On that particular night, Williams had an unusual dream that he remembered in great detail.

He dreamed he was in the lobby of the House of Commons, the lower house of the British Parliament. Williams watched in horror as a man in a dark coat with metal buttons drew a pistol. He fired the gun at a smaller man dressed in blue with a white vest who had just entered the lobby. The bullet hit the small man in the heart, and he was killed instantly.

Williams vividly recalled the sound of the gunshot and the blood that poured from the fatal wound and stained the white vest. As other people in the lobby ran and grabbed the murderer, Williams shouted, "Who was shot?"

"He's killed Spencer Perceval!" declared a man in the crowd. Perceval was the British prime minister and chancellor of the exchequer (treasury).

At this point, Williams woke up and immediately described his dream to his wife, who was still awake. What made this incident unique is that Williams fell asleep again and had the exact dream twice more that night. He dreamed three times that Prime Minister Perceval was assassinated!

Over the next few days, Williams shared his disturbing dream with his brother, his partner, and two friends who lived nearby. Six people, including Williams and his wife, were aware of the content of the mysterious dream.

"I'll go to London and warn the prime minister," he announced to his friends.

"He'll never believe you, John," they replied. "He'll just ignore the warning."

"Perhaps you're right," said Williams with a sigh. "Anyway, I haven't had that dream again since that night."

According to Herbert B. Greenhouse, author of *Premonitions: A Leap into the Future*, another man had an almost identical dream to John Williams's, although not on the same night. The dream occurred on the night of May 10, and in it the prime minister was murdered by a man wearing a green coat with brass-colored buttons.

Greenhouse wrote that "the second dreamer was Perceval himself! All week he had had a feeling that he would be killed and had told his wife it would happen very soon."

When Perceval told the Earl of Harrowby his dream on the morning of May 11, the earl warned him not to go to Parliament that day. But despite the warning, the dream, and the strong feelings that he would be killed, Perceval went to the House of Commons on May 11 anyway.

Sure enough, the prime minister was shot dead by a man named John Bellingham as he walked through the lobby to vote on a bill before the House. Bellingham wore a green coat with brass buttons! Details of the murder verified by eyewitnesses matched the dreams of both Williams and Perceval.

Greenhouse explained that Bellingham, a convicted embezzler, hated Lord Granville Leveson-Gower, a member of the House of Lords (the upper house of the British Parliament). Apparently, Leveson-Gower had ruled against Bellingham when he had reviewed his criminal appeal.

Did Bellingham mistake Perceval for Lord Leveson-Gower, his intended victim? Greenhouse thinks so. Did Williams and Perceval pick up the telepathic thoughts of Bellingham as he planned the crime? It's not likely, since if they had, Leveson-Gower would have been the victim in their dreams instead of Perceval.

Was this incident a genuine case of precognition or premonition, whether or not the killing was a mistake or intentional? Skeptics might dismiss the entire experience as an unusual coincidence. But others believe this is a well-documented case supporting the fact that extrasensory perception does exist in certain psychic individuals.

The Gypsy's Prediction

"You will die twice!" shouted the old Gypsy woman as they led her away. She shook her fists in the air. "And you will be buried twice!"

Agatha Martin ignored the Gypsy's words, as church members escorted the old woman off the rectory grounds. After all, the Gypsy had been telling fortunes and Agatha's husband, Archdeacon Martin, rector of the parish of Killeshandra in County Cavan, Ireland, would definitely disapprove.

According to D. A. MacManus in his book *Between Two Worlds*, the incident was quickly forgotten and life went on in this small, late-nineteenth-century town.

Agatha passed away a few years later. As was the custom, she lay in the open coffin while friends and family passed by. The next day, she was buried in a graveyard a half mile from the rectory. Since Agatha was a well-respected and beloved member of the community, hundreds of people from throughout the district attended the funeral.

Late that night, hours after the Martin family went to bed, there was a heavy knocking on the front door. The butler woke up, pulled on some clothes, and grabbed a lamp. As he walked to the door, the loud knocking continued. Suddenly, he froze in his tracks. The butler realized that the noise at the door was the unmistakable knocking pattern of his late mistress, Agatha Martin!

The butler shook off the feeling of fear. After all, Miss Agatha was dead and buried. He had seen her coffin lowered into the ground.

With trembling hands, the old man opened the door. What he saw filled him with unspeakable horror. There standing before him was the ghost of his dead mistress, dressed in her burial shroud, and holding a lighted candle in her hand!

Immediately the ghost began talking. After quite some time, she managed to convince the butler (and eventually the rest of

the family) that she was Agatha, and was very much alive and not a ghost.

The family vault wasn't supposed to be sealed until the next morning, and that evening some thieves broke into it. They lifted Agatha's coffin lid, intending to steal the expensive rings with which she was buried. As they began to twist the rings off the dead woman's fingers, Agatha suddenly sat up in her coffin and spoke. The thieves screamed and ran into the night, convinced they had seen a ghost.

Evidently the thieves were rough enough to awaken Agatha from the deathlike coma she had been in. Realizing what had happened, she picked up the candle the thieves left behind, climbed out of the coffin, and walked home!

After this awful experience, Agatha Martin lived another twelve years at the rectory with her husband. When she finally died, Agatha was placed in the same family vault that she once briefly occupied.

"You will die twice and you will be buried twice," predicted the old Gypsy, and that's exactly what happened. Was it a coincidence? It's impossible to know. Even today, the townspeople in Killeshandra talk about what happened to Agatha Martin so many years ago.

The Man with the X-ray Eyes

Psychics who perform onstage for money are often called mentalists. They accomplish amazing feats of telepathy and clairvoyance, but many are considered magicians or tricksters because they use illusions and other gimmicks.

One unique mentalist who astonished both psychic investigators and magicians alike was an Indian named Kuda Bux. He was known as "The Man with the X-ray Eyes."

As described in the Time-Life book *Psychic Powers*, Bux was born in Kashmir, India, in 1905. He first gained fame as a young man by walking across hot coals without apparent pain or damage to his feet. In 1935, he passed through a fire that had a measured temperature of 1,400 degrees centigrade, also without injury.

In the late 1930s, after moving to the United States, Bux became famous for his stage act of "eyeless sight." According to the editors of Time-Life Books, he "raised simple blindfold effects to a level that may never be surpassed or explained."

Instead of using simple blindfolds, through which critics might accuse him of peeking, Bux covered his eyes with layers and layers of gauze and tape. First, members of the audience placed large coins over each of his eyes and secured them in place with adhesive tape. Then other audience members spooned great amounts of flour paste over his eyes, followed by layers of cotton and more tape. Finally, a large surgical bandage was wrapped around Bux's head until he looked like an Egyptian mummy.

How did he breathe? Only his nostrils were left unwrapped, which caused one psychic researcher to question whether the mentalist could see with his nose!

With his eyes and head completely bandaged, Bux was able to copy messages, read books chosen at random by the audience, and

even describe objects held up by audience members.

Were some of the spectators secret participants in the act? Did Bux memorize the books? This was highly unlikely since newspaper reporters and psychic investigators monitored his every move, ready to expose any trickery that might have taken place.

One particular feat convinced skeptics that Bux's powers were real. He rode a bicycle totally blindfolded through heavy Times Square traffic in New York City without injury. Most agreed that few people could accomplish this without a blindfold, let alone having no sight at all!

How did Bux do it? Nobody knows. Even skeptics could not explain the mentalist's abilities. After he underwent cataract surgery, his vision became permanently damaged, but this didn't affect his act. Completely blindfolded, Bux still performed perfectly. Yet, when he removed the bandages, he had only limited vision with his own eyes.

Was it extrasensory perception, or was it trickery? If the act was a fraud, no one ever discovered how the Kashmiri mentalist was able to achieve his eyeless sight. The mystery remains to this day.

Danger at Sea

Marylee Klein and her younger sister were very close growing up. While Marylee seemed to have ESP abilities, including telepathy and precognition, her sister Ellen did not. In fact, Ellen refused to believe in her sister's abilities.

However, one evening in particular caused nonbelievers such as Ellen to wonder about the mysterious powers of the mind. Marylee described the night of August 10, 1944, in *The Psychic Reader*, edited by Martin Ebon.

Ellen was working on a top-secret project for the United States government during World War II. Even her own sister had no knowledge that she shipped out from Seattle, Washington, on the way to Hawaii on August 8, 1944.

Two nights later, Marylee was at her home in New York City when she suddenly became aware of her dead mother's presence. This wasn't unusual, since she often had contact with her mother's spirit. But what her mother said was what frightened Marylee.

"Something dangerous is happening at sea to your sister," she told her oldest daughter. By ten-thirty that night Marylee felt great fear and tension throughout her body. She told her friend Dorothy that something terrible was happening to Ellen.

The next night, the spirit of Marylee's mother appeared again. "Bombs are falling where Ellen is," she declared. Marylee focused her thoughts on her sister's safety throughout the day and night, but it wasn't until the next morning that the terrible fright she experienced went away.

"Then I knew that whatever was occurring in connection with my sister was over," explained Marylee. Yet she didn't know what it was that happened, and considering Ellen's top-secret status, could do nothing but wait for an explanation. Because of her powers of clairvoyance (the ability to know things with-

out using the five basic senses), Marylee believed her sister was still alive. But she did not hear from her for months after the incident.

Finally, Marylee contacted the War Department and was reassured that her sister was safe and stationed in Hawaii. Eventually, Ellen wrote about what really happened that night.

It took her ship, a transport carrying 1,500 troops, an entire month to travel from Seattle to Hawaii. It zigzagged its way across the Pacific to Pearl Harbor in order to avoid Japanese bombers. But the maneuvers weren't successful. On the ship's second night out, August 10, it was attacked by enemy war planes. The bombing lasted through the night and into the early morning hours.

"The bombs were practically raining from the sky," wrote Ellen to her sister. "But they never touched the ship. It was almost as if invisible hands caught each bomb and diverted it into the water."

Since Ellen didn't believe in spirits or her sister's ESP, she had no explanation for her experience. Were Marylee and the spirit of her mother responsible for protecting Ellen that night? Or was it luck that saved her from the bombs? What do you think?

Sounds from
the Past

Do past events imprint themselves on the landscape? Do disturbing incidents replay again and again to certain psychic individuals? Two women named Jane and Sally believe they do. One frightening morning they heard an entire battle that actually happened nine years earlier during World War II.

Before dawn on August 19, 1942, 10,000 Canadian and British troops attacked the German-held port of Dieppe in France. It was a long and costly battle for the Allies, who suffered more than 3,500 casualties in only a few hours.

The two Englishwomen were on vacation near Dieppe on August 4, 1951, when they were suddenly awakened at 4:00 A.M. by the sound of gunfire. For the next few hours, Jane and Sally heard the noises of a violent battle, the crackle of machine guns, the sounds of low-flying aircraft, and even the moans of the wounded.

Yet, when they looked out their window toward the sea from their small hotel, they saw only the beautiful French countryside, perfectly calm in the still morning. Did the two women get too much sun on the beach the day before? Were they sharing the same hallucination? It's not likely.

One was the wife of a member of the British Parliament and the other was her sister-in-law. They both recorded on paper the sounds of the battle they heard. Neither was likely to fantasize or have unusual visions, and it's especially unlikely for both to have had the exact same fantasy or vision.

Yet Sally and Jane listened to the sound of distant rumbling that grew louder and louder as they lay still and afraid in the dark room. "It sounded like a roar which ebbed and flowed," explained Sally. "We could distinctly hear the sounds of cries, shouts, and gunfire." Jane had served as a nurse during the war and had no doubts they were hearing the sounds of battle.

At 4:50 A.M. there was a sudden quiet, but fifteen minutes later the noise began again. The sounds of bombing became overwhelming. The women heard the diving airplanes and the whistle of the bombs as the planes released their payloads. Even the rattling of tanks was heard near the hotel.

There was silence again at 5:40 A.M. but ten minutes later Jane and Sally heard waves of aircraft flying overhead. The quiet at 6:00 A.M. turned into the moans and cries of the thousands of wounded. Finally, at 6:55 there was a total silence that lasted until the women heard the happy, chattering sounds of birds singing outside their balcony. It was then they knew the battle had ended and their strange experience was over.

After asking around the hotel, the two women discovered that no other guests in the area had heard the battle noises. So they sat down and wrote separate versions of their experience and submitted them to the British Society for Psychical Research.

Society investigators found that in comparing the women's timetable of events in 1951 with the actual 1942 invasion, the bombing attacks, periods of silence, and aircraft and tank movements corresponded almost exactly to the sequence of events in the actual battle. Yet a detailed account of the Dieppe attack wasn't published until years *after* the women's experience!

If the women had imagined or invented the experience, how could the details match the actual battle timetable revealed years later? Did Jane and Sally have a true psychic experience?

In 1952, the British Society for Psychical Research concluded that this event "must be rated as a genuine psychic phenomenon." What else could it be?

Glimpse of the Future

In cases of precognition or premonition, a person may receive an advance warning or have knowledge of upcoming events before they happen. Some rare cases of seeing things in the far distant future have also been documented. An interesting and unusual example of this type is described by Arthur Osborn in his book *The Future Is Now*, as well as by David Beaty, author of *Strange Encounters—Mysteries of the Air*.

The incident in question happened in the winter of 1935 to British Air Marshal Sir Victor Goddard, whose accuracy and integrity were considered faultless beyond question. Goddard was at the flight controls of his Hawker Hart, an open-cockpit airplane with no radio instruments. The weather was terrible—heavy rain, dense fog, and cloud cover.

Suddenly, Goddard lost control of his aircraft and plunged headlong into an 8,000-foot spin. Just as he wondered whether the Hart would crash into the surrounding mountains or the waters of the Firth of Forth in eastern Scotland, he regained control of the plane.

According to Goddard, he was at such a low altitude that a girl who was running along the open path near the water "had to duck her head to miss my wingtips."

Flying low, Goddard made his way to the Drem airfield, which had been abandoned since World War I. The old hangars were now mainly used by farmers for storing crops and machinery. The field also served as grazing meadows for local farm animals.

He saw the dark hangars of Drem in the distance through the heavy sheet of pouring rain. Suddenly "the area was miraculously bathed in full sunlight," Goddard wrote, "as though the sun were shining on a midsummer day."

As the small airplane flew over the de-

serted field, he saw the strangest things. The hangars appeared to be brand new and their doors were opened wide. Five bright yellow aircraft were lined up near the runway. Four of them were two-winged biplanes, but one was a single-wing monoplane. The biplanes appeared to be standard training craft with which Goddard was familiar. But at that time, there were no monoplanes in the Royal Air Force (RAF).

Goddard was confused. All RAF aircraft were painted a silver-aluminum color. There were no yellow planes. Yet, he clearly saw five bright yellow airplanes on the field below.

He also noticed mechanics in blue overalls wheeling another monoplane out of the nearest hangar. "The men below were not interested in me as I sped over them not more than fifty feet above the hangars," Goddard related. "I must have been making a great deal of noise. Zooming the hangars, as I was doing, was a court-martial offense!" Yet not a single mechanic even glanced up at Goddard's plane. It was almost as if he was invisible to them!

"It struck me as strange that the airmen were wearing blue overalls," Goddard continued. "RAF mechanics had never worn anything but brown overalls."

He flew out of the bright sunlight past Drem airfield and into the dark rainy mist. The Hart gained altitude and returned home safely. Goddard explained, "I knew I had been seeing things. I also knew that what I had seen was there. It was real."

Goddard told his friends about his experience and what he had seen, but they all shrugged it off. "Perhaps you should drink less of the local beverage," they said as they laughed. He came to think of the incident as a vision he had had, and continued to relate it to others, even writing down an account in a letter.

Several years passed. Because of an increase in accidents at training schools, the RAF decided in 1939 to paint all trainer aircraft bright yellow so they could be seen easier! That same year, Drem airfield was rebuilt and reopened as a flight training school. It was equipped with yellow 504N biplanes and Magister monoplanes! A change was also in store for mechanics in 1939. Now they wore blue overalls, when before they had worn brown!

Was this entire experience a figment of Goddard's imagination? It's not likely, since he told many friends the specifics of the vision and even wrote it down in a letter.

Years later, the vision became reality. "What I had seen as I flew over Drem and described to friends," said Goddard, "came to pass four years later in all its details."

Did Sir Victor Goddard fly four years into the future? Did he glimpse a view of tomorrow? Was Goddard in an entirely different realm or dimension, so as to be totally unnoticed by the mechanics only fifty feet below his airplane?

All of this seems to have happened. Yet there will always be those skeptics who will dismiss Goddard's experience as fantasy.

Bad Dream

Sometimes a dream can be so disturbing and powerful that it forces the dreamer to take immediate action. *Challenge of Psychical Research*, by Gardner Murphy, relates one such case, where a woman cut short a vacation despite objections from her husband and other family members.

In November 1952, Helen Turner of Bessemer, Louisiana, dreamed that her four-year-old grandson, Billy, was terribly ill. He was burning up with fever and seemed close to death.

In the dream, Turner's son, John, then came to the door of Billy's room, holding his hand to his head. John explained that he had fallen from a telephone pole in his job as a lineman with the phone company. When he moved his hand, blood began pouring from a hole above his eye and Turner screamed.

When she woke up, the feeling of terror from the dream stayed with her, and she couldn't get back to sleep. The next morning, Turner told her husband how disturbed she felt and insisted on returning home immediately. Her husband and the relatives they were visiting thought the whole thing was ridiculous.

Turner declared that she would take the car and go home alone, if need be. Her husband finally agreed to accompany his wife, but was so angry that the trip was made in complete silence.

After arriving home, Turner stated, "The dream I had was re-enacted completely." She went into Billy's room and found that he was very ill with a high fever. She insisted that her daughter, Janet, take him to the doctor immediately.

While they were getting ready to leave, Turner asked her daughter about John, recalling the second part of her dream. Janet said that John had gone to work as usual that morning and was fine.

Bad Dream

Sure enough, within a short time, John was brought home from work after falling from a telephone pole. He had a deep cut above his left eye that was bleeding badly. Mrs. Turner's dream had come true, exactly as she remembered it.

Both her son and grandson were rushed to the doctor. John's head wound was treated and required stitches. Billy had a severe case of tonsillitis. His fever had reached 105 degrees and the doctor succeeded in lowering his temperature. Both recovered completely.

Did Mrs. Turner have an actual precognitive dream of future events? It seems so. How else can you explain what occurred?

Mrs. Turner claimed that many previous dreams of hers had also come true. "Almost always they are of an ordinary nature, not signs of disaster like this one," she stated to the American Society for Psychical Research. "I have dreamed of relatives whom I haven't seen for years only to hear from them the next day."

Since the incident, Mrs. Turner declared, "Every night I go to bed, I hope that I will not have a dream!" How can you blame her?

Past Lives

According to public opinion polls, nearly one in four Americans believes in some type of reincarnation. Are the souls of human beings reborn into new physical bodies after death? No one knows for sure, but researchers continue to investigate the possibility.

One type of evidence that supports reincarnation is called "spontaneous episodes." These involve instances where people seem to have strong unexplained memories of what they believe to have been a prior life.

An example of this is discussed in the book *Psychic Voyages*, by the editors of Time-Life Books, which deals with the late American general George S. Patton (1885–1945). As a young captain in 1917, Patton was sent to Langres, France, to operate a tank school. He had never been there before, yet, for some reason, he knew the region very well.

"This is the site of the ancient temple and amphitheater," Patton pointed out to his astonished guide. "And this is where Julius Caesar made his camp." How could Patton have known these things? Was it his vast knowledge of military history? Or was it reincarnation—remembrance from a past life?

The town had once been the location of a Roman military camp, and Patton believed that in one of his former lives he had visited the area as a Roman soldier. The general felt that he was a warrior who died in battle many times throughout history, not only as a Roman legionnaire but also as a soldier under Alexander the Great and Napoleon.

Another type of evidence that seems to support reincarnation is referred to as "hypnotic regression." While the subject is in a hypnotic trance, he or she is taken back to childhood, and then to infancy. The hypnotist then attempts to take the subject back to the time *before* birth to see if memories exist of any past lives.

A technique known as past-life therapy is used by some psychiatrists and psychologists to deal with certain fears people have in their present lives. For example, the theory supports the belief that someone with a terrible fear of water may have drowned or nearly drowned in a past life. Reliving this traumatic experience in the previous life may help cure the problem.

One well-documented case of hypnotic regression is described in *Psychic Voyages*. A swimming instructor from South Wales named Graham Huxtable was hypnotized and tape-recorded by a Welshman named Arnall Bloxham. Under hypnosis, Huxtable became an entirely different person, named Ben, who was a master gunner on an eighteenth-century British warship called H.M.S. *Aggie*.

As Ben, Huxtable's voice grew loud and heavily accented, full of nautical terms. By asking questions, Bloxham determined that the ship was captained by a man named Pearce and was waiting to attack French vessels off the coast of Calais.

As a French ship was sighted, Ben reenacted the battle. "Steady, lads, steady," spoke the gunner to his men. "Wait for the order."

"Now, you fool. Now!" he screamed as the shots were fired. "Well done, lads. Run 'em up. Hurry, men."

Suddenly, Ben shouted, "By God, they've got old Pearce, they've got Pearce." After a pause, he screamed again, "My bloody leg! My leg! My leg!"

When Huxtable came out of the hypnotic trance, he complained that his leg hurt him. When he listened to the tape recording of the session, Huxtable was astonished at what he heard himself say.

Speech experts verified the eighteenth-century dialogue spoken by Ben. But after a thorough search through naval records, Bloxham was unable to find an actual ship named *Aggie* or a Captain Pearce. Otherwise, Ben seemed to be a real personality.

Was Huxtable reliving an event from a past life? How else could he have reenacted a scene from an eighteenth-century warship?

Cryptomnesia is a type of abnormal memory. According to *Psychic Voyages*, "subjects tap into a detailed memory of something of which, when they are in a normal state of consciousness, they are unaware."

Can material from a long-forgotten book, movie, or other source, lodged in the subconscious mind, be somehow called up and used while under hypnosis? Do all people have hidden knowledge in their subconscious memory that they're normally not aware of?

In Graham Huxtable's case, experts couldn't trace a book or movie he had come across in his lifetime that could account for Ben and his eighteenth-century naval expertise. "If Huxtable was not actually reliving a past life," say some researchers in *Psychic Voyages*, "he was certainly drawing on powers of recall or invention that are equally mysterious."

Cryptomnesia or reincarnation? What do you think?

The Next Voice
You Hear

"What was that you said?" the student pilot asked his instructor, Eddie Keyes. They were flying in a T-28 trainer airplane on a clear, starry night in the 1950s.

"I didn't say anything," replied Eddie. "Why did you say for us to land?"

"I didn't say it. You did!" explained the astonished student.

According to Martin Caidin in his book *Ghosts of the Air*, Eddie Keyes was a veteran pilot of World War II, an experienced flight instructor, a crop duster, and a mechanic. He was a no-nonsense, down-to-earth kind of guy and he had distinctly heard a voice say,

"Land." His student had also heard a voice say, "Land." Neither man claimed to have spoken, yet both heard the voice.

An alarm suddenly went off in Keyes's head. He shoved the control stick forward and dove for the nearest airfield, only minutes away. A voice had said, "Land," and that's exactly what he intended to do!

Leveling out of the dive, Keyes dropped the landing gear and wing flaps as he approached the runway. Just as the wheels were about to touch the ground, the T-28's engine exploded in a mass of flames.

Keyes braked hard and yelled to his student, "Get out! Run!" Both men jumped out of the cockpit, landed hard on the ground, and ran away from the plane. Behind them, the plane exploded in a huge fireball. Keyes and his student sat at the edge of the runway, staring at the blazing inferno, without saying a word.

Years passed. On September 13, 1964, Keyes, author Caidin, and a friend named Zack were flying a small Piper Aztec from Grand Junction, Colorado, to Witchita, Kansas, on another clear, starry night. It was 11:00 P.M. and the Aztec was passing over Dodge City.

"What?" Keyes asked.

The Next Voice You Hear

"What do you mean, what?" Caidin replied.

"You said turn right," said Keyes.

"I didn't say a thing," declared Caidin. "*You* said turn right."

The two men stared at each other, then looked back at their friend Zack, who was sound asleep. Someone had said, "Turn right," and it wasn't any of them.

Keyes quietly mumbled, "Oh, my God!" Without a moment's hesitation, both men pushed hard on the right rudder and shoved the throttles forward. The Aztec made a sharp right turn so fast that their friend woke up as his face smacked against the window. "That voice said to turn right," said Caidin, "and by God, we turned right."

Suddenly, a golden glow spread throughout the cabin of the airplane. According to Caidin: "Right where we would have been had we continued on our course, a huge flaming object hurtled down from the sky and plunged into the Earth far below." A fiery meteorite passed so close that its shock wave caused the Aztec to shake and tremble.

"Who told you guys to turn before that thing came down?" said their friend Zack, who was now wide awake and frightened. Keyes and Caidin had no answer to give him.

Mysteries of the Mind and the Senses

Twice in his lifetime, Eddie Keyes and his copilots heard a voice telling them to land and turn right. Twice in his lifetime, Keyes did what the voice told him. On both occasions, the voice saved his life!

What was it? Where did it come from? Was it the voice of God? Or did it originate within the men's own minds, warning them of approaching disaster? "We just don't know," Caidin declared.

Dream of Bill

In January 1945, a woman from San
Francisco had a dream about her nineteen-
year-old son, Bill, who was in combat in the
South Pacific during World War II. This case
was described by Louisa Rhine in her book
Hidden Channels of the Mind.

"I dreamed my son came to me while I was
busy in the kitchen," she wrote. "He handed
me his uniform, which was soaking and dripping wet." The woman began to wring out
the water from the uniform, but her son took
it out of her hands and dropped it into the
laundry tub.

He said to her with great sadness, "Isn't

this terrible! Oh, Mom, this is the one thing that I had so hoped you would never have to hear!"

Mother and son walked into the living room and sat down. Bill put his arms around his mother's neck and his head on her shoulder, and then he began sobbing.

"Suddenly," explained the woman, "he was a little infant again and I was rocking him as I had when he was a baby." The dream ended when the woman woke up with a start. It had seemed so real to her, and she was very disturbed by it.

Six days later, a chaplain from the naval base in Long Beach, California, informed the woman that something had happened to Bill's ship. His name was listed as one of 250 missing sailors.

A few days later, the Navy Department confirmed there had been an enemy torpedo attack and the ship had taken several direct hits at Guadalcanal. Loaded with tons of ammunition and bombs, the ship exploded and sank, killing all 250 aboard. The date of the attack, January 20, 1945, was the very night when the woman had dreamed about her son, Bill!

Was the dream a premonition of Bill's death? Bill was alive in the dream, but was very upset and comforted by his mother. Nothing in the dream was real, nor did it actually happen later on. Yet there was a deeper meaning to it. According to Louisa Rhine, the dream "carried a sense of tragedy." It had a mixture of symbolism as well as psychic information.

Was Bill's dripping wet uniform symbolic of his death in the water? When Bill said he had hoped his mother would never have to hear this one thing, did he mean the news of the death of her only child?

Was the transformation of Bill from an adult to a baby in his mother's arms part of the normal memory a grieving woman might have of a suddenly dead child? Or was it just a coincidence that the dream occurred on the exact night that his ship was destroyed by enemy torpedoes?

Did Bill try to visit his mother one last time? There are many questions but no definite answers.

Hidden History

William Denton, a professor of geology in the 1860s, believed every object in the universe possessed its own hidden history. In his 1863 book, *The Soul of Things*, Denton declared that people could discover this hidden history simply by holding an object in their hands. In the 1880s, this theory became known as psychometry, and it has been used by many well-known psychics such as Eileen Garrett and Peter Hurkos.

Denton conducted some amazing experiments in Boston, Massachusetts, with his wife and his sister-in-law, Mrs. Cridge. He called them "sensitives" instead of psychics, but the results were the same. They had the ability to "read" the history of each object placed in their hands.

In his experiments, Denton went out of his way to disguise the objects before handing them over to his sensitives. They were all wrapped in identical brown paper and mixed up so that even Denton himself had no idea which one was which.

When Mrs. Cridge took the first object in her hand, she saw visions of an exploding volcano and a river of lava pouring into the ocean. "I see ships on the ocean," she added.

What was Mrs. Cridge holding? It was a piece of volcanic rock from the 1840 eruption of the Kilauea volcano on Hawaii. At the time of the eruption, the United States naval fleet was visiting the area, thus accounting for the ships in Cridge's vision.

In other experiments, a piece of dinosaur bone resulted in a vision of several giant reptiles frolicking on a prehistoric beach. Mrs. Cridge also saw large birdlike creatures with wings, resembling pterodactyls.

A fragment of a meteorite resulted in an image of empty black space with large, bright stars. A piece of flintlike rock (called hornstone) from the Mount of Olives in the

Holy Land gave Denton's wife a vision of the city of Jerusalem.

In the 1890s, Denton's theory that every object carried its own history came under attack by Thomson Jay Hudson, author of *The Law of Psychic Phenomena*. He believed Denton's experiments involved telepathy or thought transference from Denton's mind to the sensitives' minds. Therefore, they were not reading the history of an object, but were picking up the information from Denton. Yet the geologist had no idea which object his sensitives were holding, since they were all wrapped alike. How could he have telepathically transmitted information he didn't know himself?

Denton firmly believed that all people were capable of being sensitives. Yet only certain people seemed to have the psychic awareness necessary to read the history of an object.

According to Colin Wilson in *Beyond the Occult*, to achieve this psychic awareness a state of total relaxation must be attained, and then taken one step further—to a total withdrawal into an inner world of the self. The result is an "intensified sense of reality" and a slowing down of "mental time."

Do all objects have a hidden history? Does

the human mind possess the ability to unravel and understand this history? William Denton believed so. If the answers to both questions are "Yes," it is obvious that most people have not yet found the key to unlocking their psychic abilities and experiencing the vast potential of the powers of the mind.

The mystery is why the limit and range of a person's consciousness haven't been investigated further by scientists. According to Wilson, that is when "the next stage of human evolution will begin." Man's final frontier may be exploring and unlocking the mysteries of the human mind.

The Flying Friar

It's been said that faith can move mountains. In the case of a seventeenth-century monk named Joseph Desa, his intense faith seemed to have given him the ability to float in the air and even fly over limited distances!

Desa's amazing story is described by British author A. S. Jarman in the book *The Psychic Reader*. Born in 1603 at Copertino, Italy, Desa was very religious growing up as a young man, and became a priest at the age of twenty-five.

The first documented case of Desa's flying took place in a church at Grotella on Christmas Eve 1628, and was witnessed by a number of shepherds. Desa became so caught up in the service that "he gave a sob, then a great cry, and at the same time was raised in the air. He flew down the middle of the church like a bird (a distance of about 120 feet), and alighted on the High Altar. The shepherds were overwhelmed with awe." From there, his reputation grew rapidly and thousands of churchgoers came from all over Italy to see the flying friar.

Once he carried a lamb as he floated to the height of the trees and stayed in a kneeling position for two hours. Sometimes, Desa lifted others with him off the ground.

The church was not pleased with this behavior and accused Desa of fraud. Yet so many testified on his behalf that he was found innocent of the charges. The Pope ordered him to the town of Assisi in 1639, but his flying fame continued as great crowds flocked to hear him conduct the mass.

Desa was transferred to one new town after another as his feats of flying continued. According to Jarman, "no less than 100 levitations were recorded by reliable witnesses."

As these events continued and his fame grew, Desa was finally brought before Pope Urban XIII. He became so excited and in awe that he floated in the air before the Pope,

who was astonished at the monk's behavior. The Pope testified officially as to what he saw, and to this day that evidence can be found in the archives of the Vatican.

During the thirty-five years of Desa's flights, documented accounts were made on the spot by those whom Jarman calls "reliable, educated, and observant witnesses." These witnesses included Princess Marie of Savoy, Cardinal Facchinetti, and the Great Admiral of Castile.

In 1645, the wife of the Spanish ambassador fainted when she saw Desa fly over her head. One Lutheran duke was so moved at the sight that he converted to Catholicism.

Joseph Desa died on September 18, 1663. According to Jarman, "even as a dying man, he levitated while the doctors attended him, remaining suspended in midair for fifteen minutes."

At the time of Desa's death, all written evidence and testimonies from eyewitnesses were collected by the Catholic authorities. The documents were filed away until 1753, when they were investigated and examined in detail. The judgment issued stated the following: "Eyewitnesses of unchallengeable integrity have testified to the uplifting from the ground and the prolonged flights of this servant of God, Joseph of Copertino."

How did Desa do it? Was it a form of mass hypnosis that made people think the friar floated and flew through the air? Did people believe he flew because they wanted to believe it could happen? Was Desa's deep religious faith and devotion the reason he could fly? Many people believed the amazing behavior of Father Joseph Desa was simply another of God's mysterious miracles.

Was it the power of Joseph Desa's mind that allowed him to resist the force of gravity and fly like a bird? Psychokinesis (or PK) is a type of psychic phenomenon whereby a person can move objects using only his or her mind and not any form of physical energy such as touching. Could Desa have used such psychic powers to elevate his own body? Perhaps, but it will never be known for sure.

Future Lives

Much has been written about the possibility of reincarnation, the belief that after death human souls are reborn into new physical bodies. Many people believe they have lived before in one or more past lives.

Hypnotic "regression" is used by hypnotists to take a subject back in time before his or her birth to determine if memories of former lives exist. But what about hypnotic "progression" and the examination of future lives? When the subject is in a hypnotic trance, he or she is taken forward in time, past physical death, to discover if future lives exist.

Future Lives

Dr. Chet Snow, in his book *Mass Dreams of the Future*, discussed the results of hypnotic progression experiments conducted from 1980 to 1988. A total of 133 subjects were hypnotized, taken forward into future lives, and questioned about life on Earth in A.D. 2100 by Dr. Snow and Dr. R. Leo Sprinkle. Dr. Helen Wambach also participated until her death in 1985. Later, 273 subjects were questioned about future physical lives in A.D. 2300.

Almost a quarter of the subjects who were questioned about life in 2100 stated they lived in spaceships or a space colony off the Earth. Those still living on the planet's surface were divided into three distinct lifestyles. Some lived in isolated modern mountain or ocean communities, referred to as New Age settlements by Dr. Snow.

Others lived inside huge, enclosed, underground or domed high-tech communities, which protected the people from the dangerous and polluted outside environment. Some resided on rural farms or within the ruins of old urban areas in a traditional nineteenth-century frontier lifestyle.

Dr. Snow speculated about what might have occurred on Earth to account for these future lives. It is likely that our continued

progress in space travel and exploration would have led to organized colonies of people living off the Earth. Nor is it surprising that planned and modern New Age communities would exist in the future, since many similar retreat settlements exist even today.

Yet what catastrophic environmental problems caused the construction of enclosed or underground cities? Was it a nuclear war or accident? What accounted for the devastation of Earth's major urban areas? Was it pollution, toxic waste, global warming, holes in the ozone layer causing harmful ultraviolet radiation? All of the above?

Or are the results of this study imaginative fantasies of what the subjects *thought* might take place in the future? Were the subjects influenced by the pessimistic predictions of today's environmentalists, who forecast continued population growth leading to decreased food supplies, starvation, worldwide depression, and widespread pollution?

A more optimistic lifestyle emerged among the subjects who reported future lives in 2300. Nearly half reported living off the Earth's surface, either in space stations, in space colonies, on spacecraft, or on other planets in the solar system or galaxy. Among those still living on Earth, the three basic groups continued into the twenty-fourth century—New Age communities, artificial enclosed settlements, and rural frontier-type towns.

The major difference between the subjects who had been reborn into future lives in 2100 and those in 2300 was a sense of optimism. Those in 2300 seemed happier, more contented, and more upbeat than those in 2100, who had a bleak and gloomy outlook.

There are questions about the research. Why would rural frontier-type towns exist on Earth at the same time as technologically advanced space colonies? One need only examine the 1990s to see how some people live lives of wealth and leisure, while others are homeless and starving.

Are the results of this study just psychological fantasies, wish fulfillments, or even the projections of inner fears of the subjects? Is there really such a thing as future progression or future memory?

Dr. Snow was first hypnotized by Dr. Wambach in 1983, and she guided him forward to the late 1990s. In a hypnotic trance, Snow described the year 1998 as being marked by the eruption of major volcanoes. These eruptions triggered earthquakes, storms, and flooding in the Far East and along the West Coast of the United States. Wambach even took Snow to the moment of his physical death sometime after the turn of the century.

Certainly Dr. Chet Snow believes in future-life progression. Perhaps you should wait until 1998 before you decide about it!

The Gift

After four days in a coma, the patient in the hospital bed finally regained consciousness and opened his eyes. He appeared confused, then frantic. "Where am I?" he shouted. "What's wrong with me?"

The nurse standing near his bed smiled. "You're in the hospital, and you're very lucky to be alive."

The patient then became aware of an awful pain in his skull. As he lifted his arm to try to soothe his aching head, the nurse said, "You fell and suffered a severe skull fracture."

The woman placed her hand on his forehead and the patient suddenly grabbed it. "You'd better be careful when you go on a train, or else you'll lose your suitcase," he said to her.

The nurse looked strangely at him. "How did you know?" she asked. "I just came back from Amsterdam on the train and I forgot my suitcase in the dining car. How could you have known that?"

The patient had no answer for her. This was just the first of many similar psychic experiences in one man's life that would never be the same after his terrible fall.

The name of the man was Pieter Cornelis van der Hurk (later known throughout the world as the psychic Peter Hurkos). His story began many years ago in Holland.

After an uneventful childhood, Hurkos traveled throughout the Far East as a sailor before he returned to his home country in the late 1930s. He was a housepainter when the Germans conquered Holland in 1940, and he joined the underground resistance movement. While painting barracks for German soldiers during the day, he and his friends stole oil, ammunition, and other supplies for the underground at night.

It was a sunny afternoon on July 10, 1941, when Hurkos's life changed forever. He lost his footing while painting a four-story building and plunged headfirst to the concrete pavement thirty feet below.

"In the three or four seconds before I struck the street, my entire life passed before my eyes, like a newsreel," wrote Hurkos in his book, *Psychic*. "I remember my terror as I fell and the one thought that was dominant in my mind: I don't want to die. I want to live!"

After he awoke from his coma, Hurkos found that he was a different man. Suddenly, he had knowledge of what was happening or had happened to other people. He looked at the man in the bed next to him and said, "You're a bad man. When your father died, he left you a gold watch and you've already sold it."

The man was astonished. "How did you know that?" he asked. "I just knew it," replied Hurkos.

Several days later, a man in a nearby room who was being released from the hospital came into Hurkos's room to say good-bye and wish him luck. As they shook hands, Hurkos suddenly knew "that he was a British agent and that he was going to be killed by the Germans on Kalver Street a few days later."

When Hurkos wouldn't let go of his hand,

the man exclaimed, "Please let me go. You're hurting me." A nurse had to come by and pry his fingers open. The man rushed out of the room and Hurkos shouted, "Stop him! He is going to be killed. I know!"

Sure enough, two days later, the man, who was indeed a British agent and had parachuted into Holland, was killed by the Gestapo on Kalver Street, just as Hurkos had predicted!

"No one can imagine how unsettling it is to see people and know all about them in an instant," Hurkos wrote. "I did not want to pry into the private lives of others, but I was given no choice at all."

Apparently, the result of the fall was the strengthening of the psychic power of extrasensory perception in Hurkos's mind. He believed this "second sight" as he called it (or "third eye," as the Dutch refer to it), was a gift from the "other world."

After his discharge from the hospital, Hurkos was determined to use the power he had been given for good purposes. As word of his gift spread, he got a job as a psychic consultant and medical researcher with a doctor in Paris. A story in *Paris Match Magazine* brought Hurkos to the attention of American scientists. They invited him to the United

States in 1956 for ESP testing and observation, and in 1959 he became an American citizen.

Over the years, he became internationally famous for his successful work on various criminal cases with police departments throughout the world. Not once during his life did Hurkos use his psychic gift for his own financial gain.

He knew the outcome of horse races, but he never bet money on them. He never played the stock market. He never gambled in Las Vegas. "I prefer to use my powers honestly, for good, and not to take unfair advantage of people," wrote Hurkos.

The man with the mysterious psychic powers died on June 1, 1988, at the age of seventy-seven in Los Angeles, California. Did he predict his own death? Probably, but Hurkos was never scared. He once said, "I would never be afraid to die again." Hurkos believed he had already died in 1941 after his fall, and that he was reborn with his special and unique gift.

A doctor who once treated him in Holland said, "There are many things about the mind we do not know and cannot explain." Peter Hurkos was a living example of this.

Collision!

According to Louisa Rhine in her book *The Invisible Picture*, a premonition or precognitive dream of disaster *can* help someone avoid that disaster if the proper preventive action is taken. Rhine describes one such case involving a streetcar conductor, who shall be called Dan.

One night Dan dreamed he was headed south on his regular route at a certain intersection. After he crossed the street, a northbound trolley passed him and Dan waved hello to the motorman. Suddenly, a large red truck cut right in front of Dan's streetcar.

The northbound trolley blocked Dan's view

of the truck and obstructed the truck driver's view of Dan's streetcar. Neither saw the other until it was too late. There was a horrible collision! People were thrown from their seats in the trolley and the truck flipped over, throwing out three passengers—two men and one woman.

When the dust had cleared, Dan saw the two men from the truck lying dead in the street. The woman was on the ground screaming in pain. As Dan ran over to her, she looked up at him and shouted, "You could have avoided this!" He remembered she had the largest blue eyes he had ever seen.

Dan woke up soaked in sweat and very upset about the dream. He couldn't get it out of his mind, even after he reported for work later that day. As Dan's streetcar approached the exact intersection of his dream, he began to feel sick and nervous. After the car crossed the street, he saw the northbound trolley at the exact place and time it had appeared in his dream.

When the motorman waved to him, Dan, now feeling very ill and nauseous, stepped on the brakes and shut off the power. Suddenly, a red panel delivery truck sped directly into the path of Dan's streetcar. If the trolley had been moving, there would have been a collision.

According to Rhine, "Three people were in the truck, two men and a woman. As the truck passed in front of him, the woman leaned out of the window and looked up at him with the same large blue eyes he had seen in the dream."

Some people believe in predestination—that no one can escape his or her fate. "It was meant to be," many conclude. Yet, as evidenced in Dan's case and with other precognitive dreams or visions, some experiences can be avoided if the warning is heeded and action is taken.

Was it a true psychic experience? Or was it just a bizarre coincidence? No one knows for sure. But Dan is thankful he took action that morning and saved the lives of two people he had never met.

Psychic Detective

Psychic Detective

The Kennedy family was picnicking at Empire Lake in upper New York State in 1982. No one seemed to notice when five-year-old Tommy wandered away from the picnic site and into the woods. When it was obvious that Tommy was lost, his parents called the Tioga County Sheriff's Office.

This case was described by Arthur Lyons and Marcello Truzzi in their book *The Blue Sense*. Deputies with dogs searched the area for seventeen straight hours without a sign of the little boy's whereabouts. Time had become a critical factor in the search. Deputies believed the boy could not survive much longer in the wilderness on his own. He had no protection from the weather, and he might have already encountered unfriendly animals.

"A deputy in the department named Phil Jordan is a psychic," said one of the men from the sheriff's office. "He located a missing boy in Bradford, Pennsylvania, last year after a two-day police and bloodhound search turned up empty-handed."

"Let's give him a try," declared Sheriff Raymond Ayers. "Maybe he can help us before time runs out on the boy."

Sheriff Ayers gave Deputy Jordan Tommy's T-shirt to hold and focus on. After a few moments, Jordan said he believed the boy was still alive. In fact, he was sure Tommy was all right and asleep under a tree!

The psychic took a pencil and paper and drew a map. Jordan drew a lake, several overturned boats, a house, and a large rock to help the deputies locate the missing boy. The Kennedys were afraid to breathe even a small sigh of relief. They wanted to believe Tommy was all right, but how could Jordan know all this just from touching his T-shirt?

Early the next morning, Jordan accompanied the deputies as they continued to comb the countryside. Less than an hour later, they came to an area that looked very much like the map Jordan had drawn. Sure enough, they found the little boy sound asleep under a tree. He was cold, hungry, and lonely, but generally in good shape.

How did Phil Jordan locate the missing boy? Most psychics who work with the police use the process known as psychometry. They receive certain impressions by handling objects belonging to the person they're trying to locate. In this case, it was Tommy's T-shirt. Not all missing persons, however, are successfully found alive like Tommy Kennedy. Some psychics have had success in locating dead bodies as evidence in criminal cases.

Many police departments are still skeptical about calling in psychics to help them in unsolved cases because they don't believe in ESP. But since the public seems to be more open-minded and favorable in its belief in extrasensory perception, more and more police departments are willing to accept help from these psychic detectives.

According to Lyons and Truzzi, a 1990 Gallup poll stated that nearly half of all Americans (49 percent) believe in extrasensory perception. Another 22 percent are not sure about it. Furthermore, a 1984 survey done by the University of Chicago found that two-thirds of all Americans (67 percent) claim to have had an ESP experience.

Lyons and Truzzi talk about a "blue sense" that good cops have. It's described as a "heightened sense of intuition that goes beyond what can be seen, heard, or smelled." The blue sense is a hunch, a warning, or a feeling of danger. This is similar to the feelings a psychic may have, though not as highly developed.

Deputy Phil Jordan has a combination of blue sense and psychic abilities. After the Kennedy case, Sheriff Raymond Ayers told reporters, "It was no coincidence! Phil Jordan simply used some kind of paranormal talent the rest of us don't have." Why and how some people have certain psychic abilities is a great mystery waiting to be solved.

Glossary

ABOLISH: wipe out, do away with.
ACCLAIM: praise, tribute.
AMPHITHEATER: an arena; semicircular curved seating around a stage.
AUTHENTIC: real, proved.
AUTOMATIC WRITING: writing by a person in a hypnotic trance whose pen or pencil is guided by spirits of the dead; also called spirit writing.

BARRACKS: buildings used for housing soldiers.

CALAMITY: disaster, misfortune.

CATARACT: abnormality of the eye that reduces vision.

CHANDELIER: a multibranched light fixture that hangs from the ceiling.

CLAIRVOYANCE: the ability to know or identify an object, person, or event without using the five basic senses (seeing, hearing, smelling, tasting, or touching).

CLASSIC: ideal, model.

COINCIDE: to correspond exactly; to occupy the same place in time.

CONFIRM: to establish what is doubtful as true.

CONSUME: to destroy, eat up.

CONTRADICTION: directly opposite a statement, thing, or proposition.

COURT-MARTIAL: a military court that tries those charged with breaking military law.

CRYPTOMNESIA: abnormal memory; detailed memory of something of which a person is consciously unaware.

DIMENSION: a measurement such as length, height, or thickness.

DIVERT: to turn aside, distract.

DUMBFOUNDED: astonished, surprised.

EBB: to drop, decline.

Mysteries of the Mind and the Senses

EMBEZZLE: the taking of another person's property or money as one's own.

EXPLOITS: actions, deeds.

EXTRASENSORY PERCEPTION (ESP): special abilities and knowledge that extend beyond the normal five senses.

FIGMENT: something imagined or made up.

FRAUD: fake, cheat.

GENUINE: real, sincere, honest.

GREENHOUSE EFFECT: the warming of the Earth's atmosphere.

HANGAR: a shelter for aircraft.

HECTIC: busy, chaotic.

HYPNOTIC PROGRESSION: while in a hypnotic trance, the subject is taken *forward* to the time after death to see if memories of future lives exist.

HYPNOTIC REGRESSION: while in a hypnotic trance, the subject is taken *back* to the time before birth to see if memories of past lives exist.

INFAMOUS: having evil fame.

INFERNO: scorching fire.

INTEGRITY: honesty.

INTUITION: feeling, hunch, awareness.

114

LEVITATION: the lifting up or floating of a medium, or others, usually at a séance.

MEDIUM: a person with special powers that enable him or her to communicate with the dead.

MENTALIST: psychic stage performer.

MERCIFULLY: thankfully, kindly.

METEORITE: any object that passes through the Earth's atmosphere and reaches the ground.

MONITOR: to watch or check on a person or thing.

NAUTICAL: having to do with ships, the sea, or navigation.

OBSTRUCT: to block.

OPTIMISTIC: dealing with the bright and favorable side of things.

OUIJA BOARD: popular board used to send messages to and receive messages from dead spirits.

OZONE LAYER: a region twenty miles up in the stratosphere where much of the atmospheric oxygen is located.

PARTITION: divider, wall.

PAYLOAD: the cargo of a vehicle.

Mysteries of the Mind and the Senses

PESSIMISTIC: dealing with the gloomy and dark side of things.

PLANCHETTE: the three-cornered device that moves over the alphabet and numbers on a Ouija board to spell out words and messages.

PRECISE: exact, definite.

PRECOGNITION: the knowledge of events before they actually happen.

PREDESTINATION: the belief that whatever comes to pass is determined beforehand.

PREMONITION: an advance warning of an event, similar to precognition.

PRY: to raise, open, or move by force.

PSYCHIC: a person sensitive to certain things that are caused by something other than the known forces of nature (the supernatural).

PSYCHOKINESIS (PK): a type of psychic phenomenon where a person can move objects using only the mind.

PSYCHOMETRY: the ability to hold an object and read its history.

REALM: territory, region.

RECTORY: the house in which a minister or priest lives.

REINCARNATION: the belief that after death

116

the souls of human beings are reborn into new physical bodies.

REMINISCE: to remember, recall.

RUBBLE: wreckage, rubbish.

SÉANCE: a sitting with a medium to contact spirits of the dead.

SEARED: burned, scorched.

SEISMOGRAPH: an instrument for recording earthquakes.

SEVER: to detach, separate.

SEVERE: harsh, strict, extreme.

SHROUD: a burial cloth.

SIMULTANEOUSLY: at the same time.

SKEPTIC: one who questions or doubts.

SOOTHSAYER: one who predicts; a forecaster.

STATUS: the state or condition of things.

SUBCONSCIOUS: beneath consciousness; the mental processes of which the individual is unaware.

SURPASS: greater than (adjective), go beyond (verb).

SYNCHRONICITY: a theory to explain events that seem to happen for a reason but are actually not related by cause and effect.

TELEPATHY: the ability to communicate over any distance from one mind to another without actually speaking.

TEMPERANCE: to stop drinking all alcoholic beverages.

TENDRILS: fingerlike spirals that attach themselves around something else for support.

TERRACED: having sloping levels or rows.

TONSILLITIS: infection of the tonsils.

TRAIT: distinguishing feature or quality.

TRAUMATIC: shocking, violent.

TRENCH: a long narrow ditch in the ground that serves as a shelter from enemy fire.

TROLLEY: streetcar on tracks that gets electric power from an overhead wire.

VERSION: a particular account of something in contrast to some other account.

VIVID: strong, distinct.

Bibliography

Beaty, David. *Strange Encounters—Mysteries of the Air.* New York: Atheneum, 1984.

Broughton, Richard S. *Parapsychology—The Controversial Science.* New York: Ballantine Books, 1991.

Browning, Norma Lee. *Peter Hurkos: I Have Many Lives.* Garden City, N.Y.: Doubleday and Company, Inc., 1976.

Caidin, Martin. *Ghosts of the Air.* New York: Bantam Books, 1991.

Constable, George, ed. *Dreams and Dreaming.* Alexandria, Va.: Time-Life Books, 1990.

———. *Psychic Powers.* Alexandria, Va.: Time-Life Books, 1987.

———. *Psychic Voyages.* Alexandria, Va.: Time-Life Books, 1988.

Ebon, Martin, ed. *The Psychic Reader.* New York: The World Publishing Company, 1969.

Mysteries of the Mind and the Senses

Editors of Reader's Digest. *Strange Stories, Amazing Facts.* Pleasantville, N.Y.: The Reader's Digest Association, 1976.

Greenhouse, Herbert B. *Premonitions: A Leap into the Future.* New York: Bernard Geis Associates, 1971.

Hurkos, Peter. *Psychic.* Indianapolis, Ind.: Bobbs-Merrill Company, 1961.

Knight, David C., ed. *The ESP Reader.* New York: Grosset and Dunlap, 1969.

Lewis, Roy Harley. *Ghosts, Hauntings, and the Supernatural World.* Devon, England: David and Charles, 1991.

Lyons, Arthur, and Truzzi, Marcello. *The Blue Sense—Psychic Detectives and Crime.* New York: The Mysterious Press, 1991.

Murphy, Gardner. *Challenge of Psychical Research.* New York: Harper and Row, Publishers, 1961.

Osborn, Arthur W. *The Future Is Now.* New Hyde Park, N.Y.: University Books, 1961.

Prince, Walter Franklin. *Noted Witnesses for Psychic Occurrences.* New Hyde Park, N.Y.: University Books, 1963.

Rhine, Louisa E. *Hidden Channels of the Mind.* New York: William Morrow and Company, 1961.

———. *The Invisible Picture.* Jefferson, N.C.: McFarland and Company, Inc., 1981.

Snow, Chet B. *Mass Dreams of the Future.* New York: McGraw-Hill Publishing, 1989.

Watson, Lyall. *Earthworks.* London, England: Sceptre, 1986.

Wilson, Colin. *Beyond the Occult.* New York: Carroll and Graf Publishers, 1988.